SMUG BASTARD

Develop Unstoppable Self Confidence And Go Screaming Past People That Hate Your Guts

MARK LLEWHELLIN

Book 5 in the
Mark Llewhellin
Success and Happiness Series

DEDICATION

This book is dedicated to the love of my life, my little miracle, Léon James Llewhellin, who I love more than anyone in the world. You are kind, thoughtful, well balanced and you are already achieving great things in your life!

Words cannot describe how much I love you and how proud I am of the person you are.

This book is also dedicated to the people who wanted me to fail, thank you for making me a stronger, more successful, and happier person.

This book is also dedicated to you the reader. Turn negativity thrown your way into the fuel you need to live the good life.

GET TWO OF MARK'S BOOKS FOR FREE

Join Mark's team for information on new books along with special offers and pick up a FREE copy of Mark's 5 star reviewed books:

'The Underdog' and 'Delusions Of Grandeur.'

Details can be found at the end of this book.

TABLE OF CONTENTS

INTRODUCTION

"No one can make you feel inferior without your consent."
Eleanor Roosevelt

"Mark, you know there's people out there that hate your guts don't you?"

This is a question that I was asked by my friend Dai O'Tool when Dai and his wife Terri-Ann came over to visit me one day. This question came completely out of the blue. And it's not something people say to me often. In fact, it's extremely rare that I hear it.

Some people may take Dai's question as offensive if that was said to them, and they may be worried about why people would dislike them.

Did I like what Dai said to me you may think?

If the truth be told, I fucking loved it!

It made me feel all warm and gooey inside because I knew exactly why some people hated me.

I replied, "Yeah, I know that."

There was a moment of silence, and then Terri-Ann confirmed what I was thinking when she said, "They hate you because they're jealous of you!"

I sat there in my chair with a big smile on my face and basked in the glory of it all. But it wasn't just any smile. It wasn't one of those smiles that says, "Hi, how are you, have a nice day." Nor was it the smile you do when someone gives you a gift.

It was a deeper, more emotionally powerful smile. It was almost sinister in nature. You know, like the one Dr. Evil gives in the 'Austin Powers' movies when he's just come up with some despicable evil plot to take over the world.

I was grinning like a Cheshire Cat, but not just any Cheshire Cat. I sat there as smug as The Cat in the Hat that had got the cream. Indeed, it was the smile of the smuggest bastard you've ever seen in your life!

The funny thing is, anybody who knows me really well will know that I'm down-to-earth and far from arrogant. However, when I feel somebody is trying to tear me down, I thrive on it!

In a kind of weird and wonderful way, I feel like I'm a

vampire feasting on the necks of those who want to see me fail because every time I succeed at something, I know I'm slowly sucking the life out of them. Like a kind of bald Welsh version of Count Dracula.

If anything, they give me more confidence, a bigger reason to succeed and be happier in life.

Have you ever come across someone that doesn't like you succeeding and being happy?

If you've been around long enough, the chances are, there'll be people who will want to see you crash and burn. They'll quietly sit there at night and watch your social media posts and see you go from strength to strength and they'll think to themselves, "Why is that bitch (or that dick) enjoying life and doing well, and my life is a pile of shit or mediocre at best?"

Watching you enjoying life, and going from strength to strength slowly drains the life out of them and rather than support you, or anyone else for that matter, it's just tears away at them.

Your success and happiness really grips their shit! It annoys the hell out of them, and they are desperate to see you fail in life. Your success and happiness burns away at them and every time they see you with a smile on your face, or every time you succeed at something, it's like you're standing in front of them blasting them with a flamethrower of shit!

Some people have insecurities and will hate your guts for no other reason than you've achieved cool things, or you've got something they haven't. I'm very different in that respect. I love seeing people doing well in life, and even when people do better than me at certain things, I'm really happy for them.

Ironically, if haters only knew that one secret to being happy in life, is having positive thoughts about other people, and wanting them to do well.

Of course if you're in a serious competition you're going to want to beat your opponent and if you're supporting a sports team, you'll want your team to win. However, there are people out there who will want you to lose, even if they're not in direct competition with you.

The main reason for this is because they feel your success and happiness highlights their failure and their dull ass life.

The good news for some of these people is they can get rid of their insecurities and can even end up being your friend, but, like it or not, there will always be some people that hate your guts.

With these people, you shouldn't waste your time worrying about why they don't like you because you've got more important things to think about, and your life is too important to give a crap about what they think.

If you have an open mind, this book will help you develop the right confidence and be more comfortable with who you are.

By having these two attributes you won't easily be rocked, and you'll continue merrily on your way into building a brighter and better future for yourself, and the people you love.

You have greatness inside you, and you have abilities and potential that are still yet to be discovered.

Read on and discover the path to a better life!

CHAPTER 1

SMUG VS ARROGANT

"There are two kinds of pride, both good and bad. 'Good pride' represents our dignity and self-respect. 'Bad pride' is the deadly sin of superiority that reeks of conceit and arrogance."
John C. Maxwell

There is a difference between being arrogant and smug, although some people may class them in the same category.

Here are the definitions of both.

ARROGANT
Behaving in a proud, unpleasant way, showing little thought for other people.
– Oxford dictionary

SMUG
Too pleased or satisfied about something you have achieved or something you know.
– Cambridge dictionary

Although the ego can be a useful thing for us when we want to achieve things, we also need to keep it in check. There's nothing that bores me so much as a person who harps on about what they've done and how brilliant they are or how they are so much better than other people.

I had that experience a few weeks before I wrote this book from a guy that had achieved a lot in the military and had served in one of the most elite units in the world. With that said, hats off to him for passing a tough course.

Sadly, my admiration for him faded away when he went on about how good he was.

I thought about a close friend of mine who had served in the same regiment (but at a higher rank) as this guy, but is different, as he's down to earth and will only tell you about certain things when asked.

My friend knows he's good at certain things and has a lot of confidence with most things. He's also very much a person who has gained confidence by putting himself out there, taking risks and fighting through his fears.

Braggers, like everyone else, are mortal. We all have strengths and we have weaknesses, and it's important to recognise that. However, there's a fine line between confidence and arrogance.

There was another guy I met one evening in a nightclub while I was doing security work for a pop-star called Sophie Ellis-Bextor.

I only looked after her for one evening so I didn't get to know her well; but in the short time I spent with her, she was polite, down to earth and was very kind to everyone she came into contact with; which was unlike the guy I'd like to talk about now.

While he was standing next to me, he gazed across the room as if he was the king of the universe looking down on all the minions in the club.

He pointed to his Rolex watch and said to me, "Do you know what that means?"

I replied, "It means that you can tell the time."

He smiled and said, "That means success!"

Fortunately, I didn't spew up everywhere, although it would've been highly entertaining if I did all over him.

This guy was beyond smug. He was smug's ugly sister... arrogant!

He was the type of person who thought he was better than other people, which is someone that I don't gravitate towards even though I knew he was trying to impress me. If anything arrogance turns me off a person.

Maybe you're the same as me, where you've got no time for people who look down their noses at others?

Ironically, he ended up in prison for swindling people out of their money in the car trade. He thought he was a winner, but his arrogance and his not giving a shit about other people lead to his downfall. He didn't care about other people's feelings, or about them getting a bum deal. All he was concerned about was filling his own pockets with other people's money however he could.

He cut corners when they put their cars in to be fixed which would lead, not only to their cars breaking down more often, but also to a potentially dangerous or even fatal situation.

Being arrogant and not caring about other people is a sure way to lose in life!

To get on in this life, it's always best to go above and beyond for people whenever you can.

If you're the person who:

Cares about other people.

Helps people.

Provides an excellent service for people.

Produces things of high quality for people.

Doesn't mess people around.

Respects people's time.

Is kind to others.

And encourages people, you won't go far wrong in life!

I remember watching an interview with Tom Jones where he was asked about successful people being arrogant and up their own asses.

Tom paused for a second and replied, saying words to the effect of,

"What you'll find is most of the biggest stars and highest achievers are very down to earth. Usually, the people who are the most arrogant are the ones trying to make it to the top."

You'll find there are people out there who just like to brag about themselves and try to tear someone else down. No matter how confident they may appear on the outside, this way of thinking can come from deep insecurities about themselves. They try to convince themselves and other people they are more important, and they somehow have one up on the other person.

They'll use phrases about other people's achievements such as, "She doesn't impress me," or, "He'll be sorry when I've made it to the top."

People with this attitude can still be successful in terms of achievements, money, or fame, but they can miss something which is perhaps the greatest achievement, "inner peace."

Regardless of whether someone is a superstar in their chosen field or whether they have achieved very little, it's still important to treat other people with kindness.

CHAPTER 2

GO FOR IT – TAKING RISKS

"You cannot swim for new horizons until you have courage to lose sight of the shore."
William Faulkner

If you want to become a more confident person, then there's no way around it, you have to take risks to further yourself.

As uncomfortable as this may seem, ask yourself the question, what is the worst that can happen if things go wrong? The chances are, you're not going to die if you screw up with most of the situations you take on.

The big challenge with taking risks is that if you fail, you're in danger of losing credibility and looking like a fool. On the flip side of that, if you take risks and succeed, then you're going to come out the other side looking better than you did before you took the situation on.

Take this book for example. I've never come across a personal development book with the same title, and I hadn't seen any books with a similar title in the best-selling charts, so this book was a risk for me. I could've played it a lot safer with a different title and a different cover.

It's possible that some people will hate this book just because of the title. Some will love it, and some will hate it, that's just the way things are. There is also no guarantee that enough people will buy the book to justify me writing it, but that's the risk I'm willing to take.

Most of the time I don't go around feeling like a smug bastard. I do however go around with a certain sense of confidence.

Am I confident 100% of the time?

Of course not.

I'm human, and I have doubts and fears just like you do in your life, but when it comes to taking on a new challenge, "nothing ventured, nothing gained."

Some people may read this book and think it's a steaming pile of shit and they've wasted their money and time reading it. This book could well sink into the realms of obscurity. But even if it does, I'm not going to sit around on my hands and cry about why it didn't do well.

Fuck that shit!

I'm writing the next book and moving on. And you should do the same with any of your ventures. Just because you failed at one thing, it doesn't mean that you are a failure. Failing that one endeavour in life is simply that, one endeavour.

You might be like me and have failed at lots of things in your life, but rather than taking them to heart, just consider it practice.

Will there be people waiting at the sidelines ready for you to fail?

Of course, but never let that stop you from trying. It's important to go beyond caring about what other people think.

Yes, there is every chance they could turn into the smug bastard or a smug bitch if you fail at something. But if you pick yourself up, move on quickly, and act like you don't give a shit, then they have no psychological power over you.

You are the one in control of your own thoughts, not them, not your friends, not your family, not any of your enemies, not any of your haters, not any of the media, no one!

You and you alone are the person who's in charge of your mind and your thoughts, and you can change your thoughts at any given time!

No inventors sit around on their hands worrying why one single experiment failed, they simply move on and keep on experimenting.

People who make it big in the music industry don't spend the rest of their lives dwelling on why one song failed; they get the next song out there and move on.

Successful actors don't have complete meltdowns because one of their movies bombed at the box office. They go out, look for extra work and try to have success with another movie.

If a builder has a deadline to finish a project such as a house and gets limited with how much time they can put into the building, from a sprained ankle, getting a cut on their finger, or they get rained off, they don't give up on the whole project. They wait it out and go again when the opportunity presents itself.

You have a glorious future out there waiting for you!

So you need to take the risks, learn as much as you can about succeeding in your chosen field and be relentless in your pursuit of success.

Just before I wrote these words I was talking to an old school friend and she told me I was quite shy in school, especially when it came to asking girls out. She was right, in fact she was one of the girls I fancied in school, but she was also one of the cool girls. So I felt scared to death with asking her out in case she fobbed me off.

I built up a scenario in my mind that if I asked her out and she rejected me, I would feel embarrassed every time that I saw her in maths class. Even if she rejected me, it wasn't a big deal, but I made it a big deal in my mind and talked myself out of asking her on a date.

Fortunately I didn't carry on throughout my entire life like that and if I did, I wouldn't have what I treasure most in my life, my son Léon.

None of us know exactly how things are going to roll when we set out on a new adventure, but you've got to take risks.

Asking someone out on a date is mainly down to how confident you are and your ability to handle rejection when it comes. Your confidence is also tied to your overall happiness. The more confident you are in every aspect of life, the happier you'll be!

Think back to a time in your life where you have taken a

risk and it's paid off.

Maybe it was:

- Trying to get a new job.
- Going against somebody in a sports competition.
- Asking someone out on a date.
- Ending an unsatisfying relationship.
- Going out on a new date that somebody has asked you to go on.
- Having a child.
- Taking on a new fitness routine.
- Starting a new business.
- Going on a plane to travel to a new destination.
- Buying a new car and hoping that it works well.
- Moving into a new property in a new area.

Whatever it is, there will be times in your life that you can look upon where you'll have taken risks, and it has paid off. So think of the risks you've taken that have paid off and decide to take some more risks.

Be bold and go after your dreams because you're the only person who can make your dreams come true!

You have the power and the ability within you to change your life for the better.

So get your shit together, and go for it!

CHAPTER 3

OUT OF THIS WORLD THINKING

"Keep dreaming big, never put the limit on your dreams, and believe that everything can come true."

Bianca Balti

Many people will limit their dreams because they are worried about looking like a fool and they worry about other people not believing in them. But if you want to achieve great things, you have to think big. And when you're relentless, and keep going with your quest, more people will believe in you and help you achieve your dream.

With dreaming big, Elon Musk is right up there.

As if co-founding 'PayPal,' 'Tesla Motors,' 'Neuralink' (a Company that aims to make devices to treat serious brain diseases) and founding 'The Boring Company' (a tunnel construction services company), wasn't enough; Elon has a dream of getting a human-being to Mars and then having a colony on Mars.

What are the reasons for this?

One of the reasons is some people think it's impossible,

and Musk loves taking on the so-called impossible challenges of life. And although many people don't worry about humanity being wiped out. The reality is, we're very vulnerable, and there are many ways that humans could become extinct.

As most of us are now aware, one of the big things that could hit us extremely hard would be a deadly virus. But if anything else happens out of the ordinary, such as a solar flare from the Sun, or a meteorite hitting the Earth, that too could also be catastrophic!

Nobody knows for sure what will happen to humanity, but if people do get to another planet, then we'll increase the likelihood of the survival of the human race.

Musk wasn't the first person to dream of getting to Mars, but when he made steps to make that a reality, many people thought he was nuts!

There is a tremendous amount of work to do before humans could get to Mars, but imagine what people would think about Musk if they were living on Mars, and he was one of the key people that made that dream a reality.

He would be classed as a legend.

Musk is the person who likes to progress in life, but not just for himself, he thinks of humanity in that way. He is concerned about the lack of progress and said,

"If you look at rocket technology it actually got worse over time. In 1969 we were able to go to the moon, and with a space shuttle we were only able to go to lower Earth orbit. Then when the Space Shuttle went away we weren't able to go to orbit, it's a negative trend line. It's not like you could extrapolate that trend line into the future and it gets good, it's a trend line to zero."

National Geographic's excellent documentary 'Expedition Mars,' shows Musk's journey with the SpaceX team, the dream of getting to Mars, and the possibility of one day colonising it.

He knew that funding would not come from the government, so it needed to come from the private company, but going to Mars turned out to be a much more difficult problem than they first thought.

When Musk first started SpaceX, he knew he had enough money for three attempts at a successful rocket launch. Although you would think at least one of the three would've worked, it wasn't to be. All three attempts failed!

So did he give up there? Hell no!

By this time, he was too far invested in his dream and was going to do everything in his power to get the money together to keep his dream of going to Mars alive.

He convinced investors to help fund the dream of going to Mars and got his chance to have a fourth attempt. But before we go any further in the story, I'd like to talk about how he got the investors to put up the many millions of dollars to fund the fourth attempt.

This could be important for you one day because one day you may want to achieve big things in your own life.

Although I wasn't there to witness it, I'm 99% sure that some of the biggest reasons that people backed him were because:

- He inspired them.
- He sold them on achieving something great.
- The investors had the chance to be part of something significant in the history of the world.
- It could also be financially beneficial to them, but they were taking huge chances with investing their

money, and nothing is guaranteed.

Most investors would like to have a financial return on their investment sooner rather than later. However, this project is an investment that wouldn't come back within a brief space of time, if ever.

On the subject of failure, Musk said,

"Failure sucks, it's really terrible, there's 1000 ways the rocket could fail and one way it could succeed; and particularly in the beginning, they tend to fail more than they succeed."

That's the same with a lot of the things we try in our own personal lives. The beginning of a new project is often the hardest time. Whether it's a new business, a new job, or a new fitness goal.

Part of Musk's genius is he's got on board some intelligent people, but not just intelligent, they can also dream big, be innovative, and keep going after big setbacks.

Shana Diaz who (at the time of writing) is the Director of Change Engineering at SpaceX said,

"We can explore the universe, we can put a colony on Mars, people can be interplanetary and it's just an engineering problem like any other. It just takes a group of people who care a lot and are happy to work hard to make that happen."

Musk knows they needed to build a series of rockets in order for them to get to the goal of landing on Mars and developing a colony. Not only must they get to Mars and land, they also have to re-launch off from Mars and get back to earth.

The rockets started off small, and when the team achieved success with one of the smaller rockets. They upgraded and tested new, bigger rockets.

This is also very relevant to our own goals.

We start with small goals, achieve those goals, and then set another bigger goal. Each time we achieve a bigger goal, it gives us more confidence. Also, the more goals you achieve, the less likely people are to be so quick to criticise you.

When people criticise others trying to make something a success, and the critics were wrong when the person succeeds, the critics are the ones that end up looking like a fool.

So what did they call this series of rockets?

They decided to the name the rocket after one of the most famous spaceships in science fiction, the Star Wars 'Millennium Falcon.'

One of the primary goals that Elon Musk and his team have is to create a rocket that is reusable.

Rockets are difficult to get to work just to go in one direction, never mind coming back. But to get a rocket to launch, go up with no glitches, come back and land is a tremendously difficult task!

When the Falcon rocket gets to its maximum altitude, it falls back through the atmosphere. Then cold gas thrusters near the top of the rocket flip it around so it's upright. After this, the stage engine fires just enough to slow its descent. As the rocket descends toward the landing site, its legs deploy and it lands.

At least that's the plan.

However, the reality of how hard it is to achieve this hit home to the team when they launched the SpaceX Falcon 9CRS-6 and tried to land it.

When it did land, it fell over and blew up!

Because the Falcon 9CRS-6 exploded when they tried to

land it, they tried again with the Falcon 9CRS-7.

The SpaceX team believed with the alternative model, they had a better chance of the rocket landing without exploding.

When they launched the SpaceX Falcon 9CRS-7, it was on Elon's birthday, June 28th. The launch was a tremendous success and people cheered as the rocket propelled itself into the air.

However, the elation was short lived, and 139 seconds into its flight, SpaceX Falcon 9CRS-7 blew up into thousands of tiny pieces!

The model after the 9CRS-7 never even got the chance to land.

This is the way it can be in our own lives sometimes.

There will be many times when we succeed and get further along in life towards our goals but then, for whatever reason, something can hit us out of the blue and set us back even further than where we were before.

In life you could take three steps forward and get hit five steps back.

Ultimately, you have to pick yourself up and have another go!

Is it upsetting, demoralising?

You bet it is.

But that's the way life rolls sometimes, and we have to accept it, dust ourselves off and get back up!

To make things more challenging, it isn't just the engineering challenges that the team has to overcome; it's also the financial challenges.

'Business Insider' estimated that SpaceX lost £250 million when the rockets failed.

The reason SpaceX wants the rockets to be reusable, is because it will be harder to establish a colony on Mars if the rockets can't be used again. So one of the big reasons for this is because of the financial cost.

For example, many rockets that go up cost around $60 million when they go up to put a satellite into orbit. And when they don't come back down, that's $60 million up shit creek!

This would be like a car company that builds a car, you

buy it, you only use it once, and then you have to get rid of it because it's no longer working.

Can you imagine the massive amount of money you would have to pay for a new car. Even a very basic car would cost a crazy amount of money and most people wouldn't be able to afford it.

Another example is, imagine you get on a plane and you go from London to New York and after that, the plane is no longer usable. The airplane manufacturers would then have to build a new plane.

Who would foot the bill for this?

You and the rest of the passengers would have to fork out the money for the costs to build a new plane.

According to Yahoo Finance, the first 747's sold at a list price of $24 million. Adjusting for inflation, that same 747 would sell today for more than $149 million.

So when we do the maths, each plane carries 467 passengers and then divide this by $149 million. This means each passenger would have to pay $319,000 for the plane to be built, and then you can add on the costs for using the airport and many other bills.

If humans are to colonise Mars, then reusable rockets are vital to the success of this mission.

On the 30th of March 2017, the SpaceX team had their fingers crossed again when they launched the Falcon 9 SES-10.

They hoped it would not only have a successful launch and flight, but it would also land successfully because this was something they still had yet to achieve.

The team held their breath as the rocket descended into the landing position and this time, it landed safely. And they made history!

This was an enormous success, and it led them onto their next goal, which was a reusable heavy-lift launch vehicle called 'Falcon Heavy.'

This is what they had been aiming for for nearly 10 years.

They knew the Falcon Heavy would be capable of getting to Mars and delivering supplies and equipment that would be needed to colonise Mars. With the launch of Falcon Heavy, they had to start 27 individual engines at the same time that would propel it into space.

It was a nail biting time for the SpaceX because there were

so many little things that could go wrong.

On 6 February 2018 Falcon Heavy successfully launched. This first goal of launching was celebrated, but it's not just about the launch that makes everything successful, it's about several steps.

This is the same as any goal that you have. It's not just about the launch of a product, a business, a new relationship, a new job, or a new physical challenge… It's about the steps of the journey and seeing that journey through to a successful finish.

The Falcon Heavy made it into supersonic flight (approximately 768 mph), and after achieving that, the first side boosters successfully broke off, and then the second side boosters successfully broke off and headed back towards earth. The plan of action then was for the Falcon Heavy to keep going into space and for the two side boosters to land on landing pad 1 and landing pad 2. It was a massive success!

The side boosters both landed successfully and Falcon Heavy kept going into space.

Falcon Heavy then delivered a payload into space, which is none other than one of Elon Musk's $100,000 cherry red Tesla convertibles.

Musk's Tesla convertible is now winging its way through space, travelling at several thousand miles an hour. It is predicted that in October 2020 it will make its closest approach to Mars, which is millions of miles away.

When you start off a goal, people will doubt you. But every time you make little successes, people will believe you more and you'll inspire more people.

So dream big dreams, be bold and take massive action!

CHAPTER 4

YOUR SUCCESS WILL MAKE SOME PEOPLE UNCOMFORTABLE

"To succeed in life, you need two things: ignorance and confidence."
Mark Twain

When you do well in life, you'll make some people feel uneasy.

However, the good news is, the ones that support you, feel comfortable in their own skin, are more confident and won't bat an eyelid. In fact, those are the ones that are more likely to cheer you on unless they feel they're in direct competition with you.

There's always going to be people that think, "Who the hell does she think she is?" Or "Who the hell does he think he is?" And will resent you for even trying to fulfil your dreams.

I had a situation in the past where one of my girlfriends said (when she found out about some things I had achieved), she felt useless and felt as if she hadn't done anything with her life.

The crazy thing about this was, she had achieved many

great things in her life. She's a lot smarter than I am academically and was the top of her class in university. But rather than look at what I had achieved in a positive light, she interpreted it into negative thoughts which made her feel bad about herself.

If I have a partner that is more successful than me, I couldn't give a monkeys.

If anything, I want to support her to even greater heights with her career and with her success.

I wouldn't feel overshadowed by her, simply because I don't give a shit if some people think she has achieved more than me.

This comes from being happy with who you are, what you have done, and being comfortable seeing other people win in life.

A win for people you care about should also be a win for you too.

You might decide that you're no longer satisfied where you are in life and want to take things to the next level.

Whether it's with losing a few pounds, hitting a certain fitness goal, starting a better job, or trying to do something that pays better; it's possible that some of your friends will want to hold you back.

If you're trying to lose weight and you're having a meal with them, they may suggest that you have the unhealthy food option just like they do. This can be because if they're overweight and they feel insecure, they may not want you improving your own body. They feel comfortable with who you are and want you to stay exactly the same.

Change can be a difficult thing, especially for people who are not willing to put the effort in to change their own lives and make their own life better. Many people, even some of your friends, will not like you moving forward because their ego may be under threat.

Maybe you do a lot for them and suddenly your focus is now going off them and you're focusing more on your own life and your own dreams.

If they are genuine friends, they will let you go on your own path and support you, even if they don't want to go down the same path as you.

It doesn't make them any worse, but sometimes they can feel worse because they think they are losing you as a friend. They can feel that way because you haven't got as many common interests as you had before. You are also becoming somebody they would like to become themselves, but they're not willing to put in the effort to achieve things because they don't believe in themselves enough.

They talk themselves out of doing better in life, so they feel they might as well try to talk you out of becoming a better person.

Ultimately, you have to follow the path that's best for you. If it's a path that can help people along the way, then all the better but never give up on your dreams because somebody tells you to.

CHAPTER 5

WHY WOULD THEY DO THAT TO ME?

"Once you replace negative thoughts with positive ones, you start having positive results."

Willie Nelson

Sometimes there will be situations in our lives that happen that will be unpleasant, and these situations are down to the decisions that other people make.

No matter how tough or mentally strong you are, there will be times in your life when people make decisions that will hurt you and you will think to yourself, "Why the fuck would they do that to me?"

I've been there myself. Whether it was from a personal relationship, from work, or where somebody was sticking their nose into my business where it wasn't wanted. I'm sure you've had all of these situations in your own life.

There can be times in our lives when we are so sure of something, and then one day out of the blue, it's all turned to rat shit and there's nothing that you can do about it!

I'd love to say I have always brushed things off within a

split second, but, just like everyone else on this planet, there are certain situations that have hurt me.

I've also spent far more time than I like to admit thinking about why a certain individual would screw me over like they did. What they did was not moral or fair, but ultimately, some people are like that, and that's the way life is sometimes.

Whether or not we like it, we have to accept the situation that has happened and deal with it to the best of our abilities.

When I've replayed the situation over and over in my mind, it's been a complete waste of time and energy and I've even had headaches and felt stressed from it.

Logically it makes little sense to replay the situation in your mind, but we're only human and this is just something that we do. So how do we get over it?

Here are some things that you can do to help you get over certain tough challenges:

- As soon as you think of the negative situation, make a conscious effort to be aware that you're thinking of that situation and replace it with something that is better and more pleasant. This isn't easy, but it can be done.

- Immerse yourself in something productive so you're not sat around all day thinking about the situation. Even if you're working, you can still think about what happened, but if you focus on the task at hand with pinpoint focus, then it will be impossible to think of two things at the same time.

- Write on a piece of paper or make an audio recording of what you would like to think about the most.

  These could be things such as:

  - Telling yourself how grateful you are for the things in your life.

    Or

  - Programming your mind with new positive thoughts.

There will be certain points in your life where you come across people that are downright ruthless and couldn't give a fuck about your feelings. As harsh as that may sound, if you have been on this earth for long enough, you will know that is the truth.

The good news is that nobody has the power to bring you down mentally, only you can do that.

You are the one that is in control of your thoughts, and you are stronger than any negativity that will come your way!

CHAPTER 6

AUSTRIAN AUDACITY

"Optimism is the faith that leads to achievement. Nothing can be done without hope and confidence."

Helen Keller

On the 30th of July 1947, a European married couple called Gustav and Aurelia had a little baby boy and called him Alöis. He was born in the picturesque European village called Thal.

Allied forces who had defeated Hitler's Nazi Germany occupied his country, and Alois' family lived in fear of Russian tanks rolling into their hometown and taking over their way of life.

Alois and his brother Meinhard, who was a year older than him, and his family attended church every Sunday. His two-bedroom home used coal ovens to heat the house and eat. His house had no shower, no plumbing, no flushing toilet, and when his family needed water, they had to walk a quarter of a mile to get it from the local well.

The water they had was limited and when they all had a wash, his mother would wash first, then his father would use the same water, then his brother, and then little Alois would wash.

Alois wasn't a huge fan of doing schoolwork, and sometimes he used to argue with his mother and try to get out of homework. Like many parents, they believed that education would help him get a better life. Despite this, there was a lot of love and affection from his Mum and Dad and Alois and his brother often used to cuddle up with them in bed.

However, if the children said something that their father didn't like, or they misbehaved, the father would hit them with a belt. In fact, one of Alois' school teachers hit his friend so hard that his head hit the desk in front of him and the child lost two front teeth!

Of course if teachers tried that stunt these days, thankfully, he or she would immediately lose their job, have a jail sentence and I'm sure that the father and mother would be in school faster than you could say "Where's my sons teeth?!"

During World War II, his father had left their hometown and become a policeman in the German Army and his Mum was a clerk. His parents in Austria were promised a better life if they teamed up with Germany, but when they lost the war things got worse for them; now there was a lot of shortages in food, supplies, and not only that, they were occupied and they didn't even own their own country anymore due to it now being occupied by the Allied forces.

Little Alois suffered with many illnesses when he was a child, but nothing that was life threatening. As a young boy, he would sell ice cream cones to people on hot sunny days and made a good profit from this. His dream was to go to America one day, because he believed that it was the land of opportunity; he told everyone that he knew including his parents, his teachers and his friends that he would go there to live. Everybody thought he was a little crazy because this wasn't the done thing.

Young Alois took more and more of an interest in building a better body for himself throughout his childhood. He took a particular interest in weightlifting and at 13 years old, he went to The World Weightlifting Championships in Vienna with some of his friends to see a weightlifting competition.

After the weightlifting competition, there was a bodybuilding competition called 'Mr World,' which was the first time he'd seen such physiques.

After the show, Alois saw a movie called 'Hercules and the Captive Women.' He was told that the main actor was also a former Mr Universe bodybuilding champion, a guy by the name of Reg Park.

Alois met a weightlifting champion that had an impressive body, he was strong, he drove a flash Alfa Romeo convertible and he had a beautiful girl on his arm; Alois wanted to be just like him.

Alois started going to the gym, and he found a new lease of life. He enjoyed the pain, the challenge and the camaraderie with his weightlifting friends. He also felt that he was starting to live his own life outside of his family and was enjoying his new independence. He read German bodybuilding magazines, but his favourite magazines were the American bodybuilder magazines published by Joe Weider.

He heard that there was a story in one magazine on the 'Mr Universe' Champion Reg Park; Park grew up poor in Leeds, England and went over to Muscle Beach in California, married a beautiful woman and got the part of Hercules.

Alois wanted to be just like Reg Park.

The magazine also featured mostly guys with hot girls on Muscle Beach in Venice, California with the warm sun beating down on them and he dreamed that one day, he would also be in California, on that very beach strutting around like a smug bastard!

He dreamed about being in California almost every minute of his waking day and didn't have a Plan B because he was determined to make Plan A work!

Alois's dream was to win the 'Mr Austria' title and then enter the 'Mr Europe' competition. His Mum felt happy that he was enjoying the new 'bodybuilding' life, but she was getting concerned at the pictures of male weightlifters, boxers and bodybuilders up on his wall.

One day his mother asked the local doctor to go round to their house whilst Alois was out and told him of her worries about her son's possible homosexuality. Fortunately, the doctor told her it was normal and that some boys have posters of people who inspired them.

When he was older Alois did national service in the Austrian Army, but his goal was not to fight in wars, he wanted to be a bodybuilding champion. However, he started winning weightlifting trophies and won one of the main powerlifting trophies in Austria and also came third in the 'Mr Austria' Bodybuilding Championships.

Alois wanted to compete for junior 'Mr Europe' but his Drill Sergeant told him he couldn't have any time off whilst he was going through basic training. Alois had a guts full of what the army was telling him to do, and walked out of the gate 'absent without leave' (AWOL) to compete in the championships, which he won.

When he got back to basic training he had to go into military jail, but his incarceration only lasted for 24 hours when his senior officers found out he had become the European champion. They loved the PR and were more lenient with him than other absconders.

He began his tank driving training but soon discovered that he wasn't a natural at it.

Routinely getting stuck in mud and having to get rescued by an 80-ton truck to pull him out. One morning he started a tank up and was testing it to see if it was running properly. He turned the engine on and started revving it up while it was in neutral. Or so he thought. What he didn't realise was the tank wasn't in neutral and he drove it straight into a wall!

When the Commanding Officer saw the mess the tank had caused in the workshop, shit hit the fan!

Despite one or two mishaps in the army, Alois was succeeding in a big way within the bodybuilding world and was featured on the cover of several magazines. By the time he was 18 years old, he had 19-inch upper arms. Even though he knew that the army wasn't for him, it still brought many benefits and he enjoyed some aspects of the discipline, the camaraderie and the physical training.

He was supposed to stay for three years, as that was the minimum tank drivers could serve.

He also enjoyed having a sense of independence away from his family and knew if he could do it with the army, he could do it anywhere. Alois left the Army and moved to Munich in Germany, where he had taken a job but couldn't afford to rent an apartment, so his boss put him up in his house.

He told Alois that he could crash on the couch and when Alois got on the couch that night, his new boss climbed on the couch next to him and made sexual moves towards him. Alois jumped off the couch and ran like fuck! He never stayed with his boss after that, but his boss still kept him on with work because he knew that he was valuable in the gym.

Alois set his goals high for his next competition and decided it was time to enter the 'Mr Universe' competition in London. Many people thought this was taking it too far, and he was punching well above his weight, but although he didn't expect to win, he wanted to see how he would place on stage with the more experienced competitors.

He also made sure that he associated with like-minded people and one of his main training partners and one of his best friends was a guy called Franco Columbu, who had won the European Powerlifting Championships.

Alois hoped that he would place in the top six in the 'Mr Universe' tournament. He knew that he wasn't going to win because of his lack of experience and that the other guys appeared to be in better shape than him, but to his amazement he ended up coming second!

He was understandably smug about this because he had so many people doubting that he could do well in bodybuilding.

He knew he needed to 'up his game' and even though he had a successful podium finish in the amateur 'Mr Universe' under his belt, it would be the only time he competed in it. Alois had already set his sights on the prestigious 'Mr Olympia' title (The biggest bodybuilding prize in the world).

Did he win every competition that he entered?

No.

But he knew that if he went in with a winning mindset, he would have a much better chance of coming out on top, or at the very least ranking high in the competition.

When one judge from the 'Mr Universe' competition invited him to stay with him and his family in London, Alois jumped at the chance. Alois wanted to move to a big city, and he knew it would take him a step closer to his dream of becoming the top bodybuilder in the world and getting into the movies.

Alois was not in a much better location, but he was living with a bodybuilding judge called Wag Bennett who would help him perfect his physique. Wag's wife Diane also told him he needed to adjust his attitude because when he would finish on stage, he was rude to fans and not give them any time. He would just push past them so he could carry on doing whatever he was going to do that night.

She told him that the fans were there to see him; he needed to be kinder to them and spend more time with them if he wanted to build his profile and his fan base.

Living in London would also improve his English speaking.

On that trip he met his bodybuilding idle Reg Park and was completely star struck by the three times 'Mr

Universe' winner and star of 'Hercules.' Alois made a clever move and went to Belfast to appear alongside Reg Park in a show of strength, and the audience loved it!

He felt frightened to do any public speaking but Reg helped him, and after he said a few words, the Irish audience loved him, which built his confidence massively.

Alois studied everything about Reg Park; he studied the way he walked and the way he talked. He left no stone unturned with learning off people he wanted to emulate. One year later he had put on 10lbs in muscle and won the professional 'Mr Universe' title. He was only 20 years old!

You may have already guessed that Alois has a longer name… Arnold 'Alois' Schwarzenegger!

Arnie then went to South Africa with Reg and Reg's family for three weeks.

He was doing calf raises with 300lbs, which he considered a decent amount of weight, but he was blown away when he saw Reg doing the same exercise with over 1,000lbs. Reg's calve muscle development was in a different league!

When Arnie saw Reg's training regimen it mentally took him to another level. He added more weight to shock his calves into more growth and eventually he was lifting like

Reg.

Arnie knew to win the other major competitions around the world he would need to be dedicated to his training, so he prioritised his training above work, recreation, travel and girls.

He trained 4 – 5 hours a day for 6 days a week!

When Arnie won the professional 'Mr Universe' title in London the next year he got a telegram from the founder of The International Federation of Bodybuilders (IFBB) founder Joe Weider that invited him to Miami for the American 'Mr Universe.'

"You will go on to become the greatest bodybuilder of all time," Weider told him and he covered Arnie's expenses for the trip, as this was back in the day when he didn't have much money.

Arnie came second in the American 'Mr Universe,' which disappointed him, and he felt like a loser.

What annoyed him greatly about coming second was, he knew in his heart that he didn't diet as he should have, he didn't train as he should have for the week prior to the contest, and he thought he would win off the back of his previous win.

He knew that he had become complacent and slacked off, and that's why he came second. It frustrated him so much that he vowed he'd never do that again!

After his loss, he focused on being in a new country with no real friends, he was away from his family, he didn't know if he had a job to go back to, he didn't speak the language and he had virtually no money. When he focused on all of these things, it made him depressed. Fortunately, Arnie was sharing a room with a guy that told him that he would win next year, which meant a lot and lifted his spirits.

Although this lifted his spirits, Arnie admits in his autobiography 'Total Recall' that he cried that night.

The next morning Arnie met up with his idol, Joe Weider, which put him on a high again. After Joe interviewed Arnie, he told him not to go back to Europe and to move to California. He offered Arnie an apartment, a car and living expenses, so he could concentrate on his training and Joe told him again, "You're going to be the greatest!"

All Arnie had to do was to give interviews for Joe's magazine, so people could learn the latest and greatest training techniques for themselves. Just one week later Arnie crashed his friend's car, his leg was injured, but it wasn't a terrible accident and his friend paid for medical expenses, which Arnie later paid back.

One of Arnie's big goals was to become a successful businessman and every opportunity that he got, he would follow Joe Weider around. When Joe went into business meetings, whether it was New York or Japan, Arnie would follow.

The man that really dominated the bodybuilding industry at the time was a Cuban called Sergio Oliva and Arnie knew that if he was ever to become the top bodybuilder in the world, this was a man he had to beat.

Sergio was pretty relaxed and didn't mind inviting Arnie over so he could see him train. To Arnie's amazement, he found out that Sergio Oliva trained even harder than he did, but instead of being deterred, it inspired him, and he knew that he had to up his game yet again!

Arnie knew that to get the best results for himself, both psychologically and physically, he needed his friend and training partner Franco Columbu in the United States with him. He loved being around Franco and also knew that Franco would push him in the gym, so he would get the best results possible.

He convinced Joe to bring Franco over and from that point on he pushed his body to new levels.

Around this time, Arnie also found out that the one time actor, Ronald Reagan, had moved into politics when he became the Governor of California and then later, Reagan became the President of the United States of America.

Whether or not he was consciously aware of it, Arnie also realised that somebody could move from being successful at one thing to another domain, which is something that he did later on in life when he also went from acting to becoming the Governor of California.

Arnold's first outing in the professional 'Mr Olympia,' resulted in a loss to Sergio Oliva. However, Arnie wasn't deterred and knew he was improving all the time and that his time was going to come.

Joe Weider also did everything he could to get Arnie the lead role in the film 'Hercules in New York,' as the producers wanted a muscleman in the part.

The role was originally going to another bodybuilder, but that bodybuilder promoted a different bodybuilding organisation that wasn't owned by Joe. Arnold was basically Joe's product, so Joe pushed and got Arnie the part because the movie producers respected the Weider Corporation and the professional opinion of its charismatic CEO Joe.

Arnie had no acting experience and admits that he found the whole thing rather daunting.

Joe had told the producers of the movie that the young 22 year old Arnie (with no acting experience) was a Shakespearean actor in Austria (Arnie later confessed that there's no such thing in Austria).

Arnie needed a star movie role, even though it was a low-budget movie. He thought he would have taken until he was 30 years old, but the Gods were smiling on him, so he took the opportunity, jumped in at the deep end, and play the character's role to the best of his ability.

Although Arnie might not have had a lot of technical acting experience, what he had was a lot of confidence, and that made all the difference!

And of course, confidence is gained by success building upon more success.

Arnie also went to college so he could improve his English as he knew he needed to be fluent to succeed in the USA; he found language learning difficult, but persisted and overcame his doubts. He also took business classes, which complimented what he had learned with Joe.

He wrote down his goals, but they weren't just airy-fairy

goals such as "build more muscle," or "make more money." He wrote goals that were more specific, such as what type of training he would do that day, the courses he would do, and the lessons he would take to further himself.

He had the same mindset with details when he looked at his posing routine. His goals would be specific and detailed and that made an enormous difference to him becoming a success!

The more Arnie succeeded in his competitions, the more the offers came in. He even had a tempting offer to make $200,000 a year to manage a chain of gyms, but he declined. It was a lot of money to him back then but he declined because he knew it wouldn't get him closer to achieving his major goals, which were winning 'Mr Olympia' and acting in movies.

Whenever Arnie finished the competition, he would always seek the judges to ask them how they scored him (i.e. what his weak and strong points were), so could build an even better body.

While in the USA and training for a 'Mr Olympia' contest, Arnie's father suffered a stroke and shortly after died. He also lost his brother in a car accident.

Although he wasn't as close to his brother and his father like he was to his mother, he wanted to make his mum's life as good as possible, and he worried about her because of how devastating those two losses were to her.

Arnie also became a successful real estate investor before he had vast amounts of money in acting. With acting, he had a specific idea of which acting part he wanted, and what role he wanted to play in movies. Because he already had made some money in property and didn't desperately need the cash, he wouldn't take any acting roles that he didn't think were suitable. He also didn't want to be playing an on-screen villain that would go around killing people, which is now ironic when you look at the first Terminator movie.

Arnie's first movie after 'Hercules in New York' was 'Pumping Iron' which is about bodybuilders training for the 'Mr Olympia' event.

However, after they made it, it was on hold and was struggling to get released. So in the meantime he did another movie called 'Stay Hungry,' which he starred in with Sally Field and it got nominated for a Golden Globe award!

Nobody expected him to win a Golden Globe, but when he won Best New Actor, the applause was led by none other than Sylvester Stallone, who was also up for a nomination for his first Rocky movie. That is where one of the most famous (friendly) rivalries in movie history began!

Not long after that, he started dating Maria Shriver, who is well known in America and is part of the Kennedy family who are very influential in the political world. Arnie found it refreshing being with Maria because she was also very ambitious. And unlike most of his other girlfriends, she believed in him, and believed that he could make his dreams a reality. Maria knew that her family had achieved great things and all of that stemmed from her grandfather who was penniless and made his wealth in both alcohol distilleries and real estate.

Maria's mum Eunice Kennedy Shriver had created the Special Olympics and her father Sargent Shriver was the major driving force behind the Peace Corps and many other endeavours. Her uncle Robert Kennedy was the 64th United States Attorney General and a U.S. Senator. Her other uncle Ted Kennedy went to Harvard and also became a Senator.

Her other uncle was John F. Kennedy, who became the youngest President of the United States of America and also told everybody in 1961 that they would put a man on the moon before the end of that decade, which America managed to do.

Maria knew that dreams became a reality when people persisted, even against impossible odds.

Arnie was asked to lose weight for a movie part because the director thought his size overwhelmed the rest of the cast and he had to lose 40 pounds. A lot of bodybuilders would have refused to do that, but Arnold felt that it was the right time to go into movies and was willing to do whatever it took. It wasn't ideal, but he accepted it because he knew he had to change to achieve his next ambition of becoming a movie star.

The director said if he didn't come down from 250lbs in weight to 210lbs, then he would not get the job. So Arnie looked in the mirror and visualised himself as a more athletic type of person and backed off on eating so much protein. He also did more running, swimming, and cycling, and cut down on the weight training.

Arnie admits that he had times in his life where he thought things were getting too tough and intense. He was working on a mail order business, doing his acting classes, going to college, working on his construction business and also training every day. He felt overwhelmed, so he got into meditation because he knew he needed to unplug and disconnect the mind for short periods, which he found beneficial.

Before a serious relationship with Maria, Arnie had a girlfriend which was his first true love but as he took more of an interest in acting, she moved out and no longer wanted to be in a relationship with him, which hurt him deeply.

Even though this was a big setback, he still managed the emotions he felt. When actors play certain scenes, they have to act out certain emotions. The first one that comes to mind is crying, where actors think of sad circumstances and it brings on that emotion.

When you want to succeed at something, rather than doubt yourself, think back to a time when you've overcome something and succeeded. You need to put yourself in a state of mind where you tell yourself nothing can stop you and it is already a given you will win!

Arnie once met an agent who insisted that he should take only minor roles in films that would attract a bodybuilding fan base. Despite being financially lucrative during his early acting days, Arnie knew that this agent didn't buy into his vision of him being a leading man.

He wanted an agent who would promote him and tell the world how good he was. He needed an agent who told producers how beneficial Arnie would be to their movie as a lead man.

Even if he didn't get the lead man role, Arnie always wanted to be one of the top three actors in the movie. However, when he tried to get in with the big agencies, they didn't take him seriously and didn't want to take him on.

One agent said:

- You have an accent that scares people.
- You have a body that's too big for movies.
- You have a name so long that it wouldn't even fit on the movie poster.
- Everything about you is too strange.

Arnie said in his autobiography, "Why should I give up my goal because a couple of agents turned me down?"

He knew he could do something about his accent and he met an elocution coach that told him he didn't need to get rid of his accent completely, but just needed to soften it a bit, so it didn't sound as threatening. Arnie spent a tremendous amount of time working on his accent and toning the harsher German/Austrian accent to a softer, friendlier accent.

As time went on, he went from struggling to getting good roles and more studios offering him better roles and not just playing 'the muscleman.'

He also set a goal to become one of the top five leading men in the film industry.

Arnie had a unique way of looking at things and said in his autobiography, 'Total Recall,'

"People were always talking about how few performers there are at the top of the ladder, but I was always convinced there was room for one more. I felt that because there was so little room people got intimidated and felt more comfortable staying at the bottom of the ladder. But in fact, the more people that think that, the more crowded the bottom of the ladder becomes; don't go where it is crowded, go where it is empty. Even though it's harder to get there, that's where you belong, and that's where there is less competition."

His dream was to be in the same league as the leading men before him such as Clint Eastwood, Charles Bronson, and John Wayne and he believed 100% that he would achieve his goal!

He was given the script for a new movie which he liked the sound of. But it was different to the parts and films he was used to so he met the new director that had only made one movie, which was called 'Piranha 2.'

The director's name was James Cameron.

Of course, Cameron went on to direct other successful movies such as 'Alien,' 'Titanic,' and 'Avatar,' but back then, he wasn't such a big deal in the movie industry.

Arnie initially wanted to play the lead role of Kyle Reese, who was being chased by the Terminator, but Cameron tried to convince him that he should be the Terminator. Arnie wasn't convinced because the terminator only had about 18 lines in that first movie, and he thought he would be taking a backward step.

His agent also disagreed with Cameron and said that Arnie playing the villain would be career suicide!

However, James Cameron stuck to his guns and of course later convinced him to play the 'bad guy' role. This was the role that made Arnold Schwarzenegger into a superstar!

When Arnie first started in Hollywood, many people thought he didn't have much depth to his acting, and that his size and his accent would hold him back from success. Ironically, all the faults that the (so called) experts in the industry said would hold him back, became huge assets to him when he finally ended up playing the Terminator!

The filming on the set of Terminator was tough at times, because of the long hours, and there were a lot of night scenes which were filmed in the early hours of the morning. Arnie said the set wasn't the happiest in the world, but it was very productive.

He disagreed with some aspects of James Cameron's script and said he should say, "I will be back" rather than, "I'll be back."

However, Cameron told him he would stick with "I'll be back," even though Arnie thought it sounded a bit feminine. This argument continued for a short while until James Cameron got to the point of saying, "Look, just trust me okay. I don't tell you how to act, and you don't tell me how to write!"

When it came time to promote his new movie, Arnie would take as many interviews as he could from the biggest international media corporations to the smallest local newspapers. Whenever he had time to fit it in his schedule, he would do it because he was so hungry for his movies to be a success.

Here's some things we can learn from The Arnold Schwarzenegger story:

- If you have a big goal, some people will think you are crazy and you won't achieve that goal.

- Visualise what you want to achieve.

- Talk to yourself positively (i.e. I am a winner, I am the best, I am a champion).

- Put the required effort in.

- Get around people that can help you with your goal.

- Read information that can help you in achieving your goal.

- Don't let anybody dilute your vision.

- Know your true value.

- Know where you're going and don't let anybody derail you.

- Having the right contacts can change your life for the better.

- Everybody has fears and doubts at times.
- Grab opportunities when you can even if you don't feel 100% prepared.
- Confidence brings you more opportunities.
- You can push yourself further than you think.
- Surround yourself with champions.
- Never think the champions you meet are better than you.
- Believe in yourself.
- Be humble enough to take advice off people who know what they're talking about.
- Don't get complacent.
- The little details can be important.
- You won't always be right.
- Be willing to travel if it's required to take you closer towards your goal.

- Just because you've lost something, it doesn't make you a loser.

- Know that it's ok to be a smug bastard, but be a polite smug bastard.

- If at first you don't succeed, try, try again!

CHAPTER 7

BE PROUD OF YOUR ACHIEVEMENTS

"Be proud of your accomplishments."
Dolly Parton

There's nothing wrong with having excessive pride in your achievements.

And I have to admit to myself that I can be a smug bastard, but this only ever emerges when people have tried to bring me down and I've come through the other side winning.

In fact, people not believing in you can be a major source of motivation.

Some people think you should shy away from being smug, but you should feel good about what you have accomplished.

You can't tiptoe around it. If you're good at something, you're good, and you should never apologise for it and you should never be embarrassed if you've succeeded at something.

You don't have to go bragging about your achievements to be proud of them.

On a personal note I find it uncomfortable to brag about my achievements because I feel:

- It's not cool.

- There's nothing to be gained from it (apart from people thinking what a dick you are).

- It's of no value to other people.

It's also important that you are proud of how far you have come since you first started your journey.

One of the things that happens to most goal orientated people is they achieve one goal and immediately set another one.

There is nothing wrong with this, and if you wish to mentally grow and make creative progress, then this is something you'll have to do.

However, sometimes it's important to take a moment and really just appreciate every good thing that's happened in your life and be grateful for how far you've already come.

The chances are you've already achieved far more than you give yourself credit for.

There may be areas in your life where you're disappointed that you haven't done better, but you must also realise what has happened has happened, and that's in the past.

As long as you can use the knowledge of your past mistakes and failures productively and take action towards making things better, then your time will not have been wasted.

There are certain things that you want to happen that don't happen, no matter how positive you are, and no matter how much effort you put in, but that's ok.

If this happens, it just means there's a bigger plan for your life.

If a relationship has failed or you've lost your job, it doesn't mean it's the end of the world.

As upsetting as some of these things can be, there is a reason, and the end of one thing can lead to something much better.

I'm working on another book where I interview high achievers that have excelled in their chosen field. It's a mixture of top sports achievers, millionaires, Olympic athletes etc.

When I was interviewing these people, I didn't have a steady 9 – 5 job and was struggling financially. However, by scraping through financially, these interviews led me to meeting many amazing people so I could learn off them and they also became valuable contacts later on down the line.

Several years ago I wanted to interview someone who was in the Special Forces that agreed to do an interview. However, he wasn't great at getting back to me with dates and times; which is something you may have experienced with your own life.

Sometimes people promise one thing and they don't back up what they're saying and they let you down.

Several days later, the lads from the SAS Who Dares Wins Channel 4 series agreed to do interviews which couldn't have worked out any better.

It was perfect, because many people already knew who these guys were, and it was much better getting those interviews than the SAS guy that didn't have a public profile who was useless at getting back to me.

My Mum had this great phrase that you she used to say to me when things didn't turn out, which was,

"Everything will turn out for the best in the end."
Diana Beckerleg

CHAPTER 8

NO NEED TO SHOUT FROM THE ROOFTOPS

"The superior man is modest in his speech but exceeds in his actions."

Confucius

This chapter relates to the chapter about 'Smug vs Arrogant' but I decided to expand on it because of its importance.

There's some debate about whether it's a good or bad thing and where you cross the line between being big headed or bragging about how good you are, keeping it real and being down to earth.

For me it's a case of just being polite and kind to people and not trying to put people down by trying to make yourself look better than them.

It's far better to praise people and help them do well in life.

There is a contradiction in our minds between saying "I want to be someone special and important" and "don't get above your station."

We all want our views to count and have a certain amount of respect. That's just a part of human nature.

No one likes to give their opinion on something and be dismissed out of hand.

Most people don't think that someone else is a better person than them, so this battle in our minds starts with conflicting thoughts of what the world wants us to be, and what we want to be.

We have big dreams and goals but if we tell certain people about them, they don't like it and feel threatened.

"Who does he think he is? He's away with the fairies!"

"She's so up her own arse, she thinks that she can achieve so and so but she'll never do it!"

This is the way some people are, when they see that you have a goal and a dream they will immediately try to bring you down to earth with a bump and try to put a stop to your so called "silly thinking."

Part of this is because they may be your (so called) friend.

They will have spent lots of time with you and they will think that you're no better than them so they may resent you achieving more than them. They think why should you achieve something really cool, and they don't?

They have a psychological label on themselves that says, "I'm going to be just like everyone else, and that's the way life is."

They believe people who achieve great things are from a different breed, have almost supernatural abilities or get everything based on pure luck.

They are partly right, there is always a bit of luck with certain things.

I'm lucky that I wasn't born with certain disabilities that would have stopped me from running otherwise I would never have achieved many of the things I have.

Not that disabilities always stop you from achieving great things.

Just take a look at Paralympic athletes or Stephen Hawking or John Foppe and Nick Vujicic who were born without certain limbs but went on to live successful lives. They weren't just successful, they also became top people in the world of helping people overcome their own fears and challenges.

Some successful people disregard luck altogether, try to give themselves 100% credit for everything, and say that it's all down to their hard work.

The reality of the situation is, it's a bit of both. But the good news for us is, even if we haven't been born with everything in the world going for us, we can still make things better for ourselves and become something greater than we were before.

When people are born into a rich country like the U.K., the United States, Canada or Australia, we sometimes tend to forget how lucky we are to have been born here.

If you're born in a developed country then you're born with a head start for many things in life.

A Statista survey done in 2020 states that 41% of the world still aren't Internet users.

Northern Europe ranks first with a 95% Internet penetration rate amongst the population and the countries with the highest Internet penetration worldwide are the UAE, South Korea and Denmark.

The country with the lowest Internet usage is North Korea. No surprises there.

Asia is the continent that has the largest number of online users, which at the time of writing is over 2 billion and Europe is placed second with almost 705 million Internet users.

Bang! Instant access to huge amounts of information. How lucky are you?

What is true about high achieving people is they are normally more focused, have more drive, and have more persistence than most other people.

As a human being, it's very easy for us to feel the need to be important.

It's one of our most powerful inherited traits, but just because we want to feel important, it doesn't mean that we have to tell the world that we're important.

When I decided to co-author some of my future books with people, I don't really care whose name was on top.

In other words, I didn't care who looks like the main person that was writing the book.

Okay let's face it, Llewhellin is a long ass name, and whether you're on the top or you're on the bottom, you're going to have quite a bit of real estate on the cover.

But even if my last name was much shorter, I was still comfortable with having my name on the bottom.

That way nobody's ego gets involved, if anything, some people I'm co-authoring with ask me if I would like my name on the top.

So don't feel too threatened by others.

There are many people out there, that can't wait to interject in a conversation as much as they can because they are desperate for people to hear them speak.

They want to feel their opinion is valued and it makes them feel more important by having their say.

When you gain a certain amount of confidence you'll be quite happy to let the other person rabbit on for a certain period of time.

Of course if they go on and on and on, as some people do, it can get a little bit tedious listening to them.

Many of these people don't realise, they won't gain as much respect off others if they are constantly blabbing on about their opinion or how good they are.

There's a very good Chinese saying that goes…

"Man with head in clouds and feet firmly on the ground is very big man."

Many of the problems in the world, whether on an individual level, or on a country level, come from having too much ego and too little self awareness.

You'll see it on the type of TV show where people are brought in to have an argument with each other and throw around blame for the next half an hour.

You know the type I mean.

There are are also people out there who may never appear on that type of show that are what's considered a higher social class, but they operate with a belief of, "I live in a certain area and drive a certain luxury car so I'm better than you."

They struggle to listen to others and it's their way or the highway.

They always feel they're right about everything and they detest saying the word 'sorry.'

Whether these people realise it or not, they are operating out of a very low level of consciousness.

No one likes to admit they're wrong, or have done wrong, but having the humility to know when you are wrong is a great quality to have.

To be the most effective person you can be, you have to think about what the other person's point of view is.

Now don't get this confused with the head political leader from certain countries.

The reason I say this is because pretty much every government leader is stuck in his or her countries point of view and that view can sometimes be to help the people in his or her country.

Of course the leader of a country's role is to help the people of the country but as history shows us it can be more about what benefits them as an individual or what benefits people in the way of money. Wars over oil and other assets come to mind.

We're all born into a country and labelled as British, American, Canadian, or whatever country you're from, and obviously support our home team which is natural.

But there comes a point where you have to go beyond the limiting beliefs of patriotism.

There is a higher level where you think and care about people beyond, race, religion, nationality, colour etc.

Ultimately, being kind, not bragging and being quietly confident will get you much further in life!

CHAPTER 9

PRAISE

"Your depression is connected to your insolence and refusal to praise."
Rumi

There are 5 categories of people who first come to my mind when I think about being praised.

- People you look up to.
- Close friends.
- Your peers.
- The public.
- Loved ones.

When I first joined 29 Commando, I wasn't in the top 10% for fitness. In fact, I wasn't even in the top half when it came to fitness.

The reality was, my fitness was poor compared to a lot of Commandos when I was younger, and in 29 Commando I was probably in the bottom 20% for my speed and endurance.

Over the years in 29, I got a little fitter but nothing significant. Towards the end of my time in 29 Commando, when the lads went out for a run, I managed to stay in the top ten with runs that were about 6 miles long.

Back then, I still hadn't found the distance that I would excel at. That was only to happen after I left 29 Commando when I discovered ultra distance running.

I admire the really fit people in 29, and as I mentioned in my book 'Delusions Of Grandeur,' my friends Marshy and Beastie were on a different level to most of the other lads in 29.

There were a few other people that were also exceptionally fit, but it was Marshy and Beastie that I looked up to the most.

When I finished the last draft of 'Delusions Of Grandeur,' I sent it off to Marshy before I published it to make sure that he felt happy with what I said about him.

What I didn't expect was a voice message on WhatsApp from him.

"Mate your book, Fucking brilliant mate! Really, really,

really good. I'm impressed mate!"

Marshy thanked me about what I wrote about him and finished by saying, "You're a good author; who would've thought it eh, ol' Taff Llewhellin 7 Battery, he's now an author, fantastic mate, fair play to you!"

I'm not one that goes looking for praise, far from it.

However, when Marshy said those words it meant a lot because I knew that Marshy wasn't the type of person that would tell me something is good, if he didn't think it was.

Marshy is very respected, and a high achiever, so it meant a lot to me that he would say such kind words.

Somebody else that I really looked up to in 29 Commando was my old Battery Sergeant Major Bruce Saunderson.

One day I scrolled down my phonebook to see who I haven't been in touch with for quite some time. Bruce's name came up, so I gave him a bell.

We had a good old chat, and one of the things that Bruce said to me was, he couldn't believe what I have achieved since I left 29 Commando. He said words to the effect that he thought it was a miracle.

This made me laugh because Bruce knew that I wasn't the keenest and greenest soldier he knew.

In fact, if anything, I would always shy away from sticking my neck above the crowd.

I just wanted to do my job, have a laugh with the lads, travel, and get paid.

I had no interest with making a career in the Army, and the last thing I wanted to do was be somebody that had to talk in front of people.

I also didn't like telling people what to do and wouldn't have enjoyed giving orders.

Although I laughed when Bruce said those words, because both he and I knew what I was like, it was also nice to hear him say such kind words and that meant a lot to me.

Not only do I respect Bruce as a soldier and a leader, but I also respected him more than most high ranking soldiers because Bruce never abused his power and he was always fair to people under his command.

It also means a lot to me when I get nice reviews from readers on Amazon about my books.

Even though I'm tough mentally, I'm also only human and we all need a bit of encouragement at times.

When I read excellent reviews off readers, and know that my books made a difference in people's lives, it gives me more encouragement to produce more high-quality books for people.

Some authors only read their positive reviews, some authors just look at the negative reviews and some, like me, look at both.

Some authors look at their negative reviews and they can be deeply affected by these reviews. Some people even quit because of them.

It's great when you get positive encouragement from people because it can give you more energy to produce more work, but at the same time, you can't let negative comments drag you down!

When I visit my Mum, sometimes she'll make me food and I will thank her for it.

She usually replies and says (in a depressing tone), "Well it's nothing much."

My Mum is set in her ways and she keeps saying this all

the time.

Rather than drag herself down, it's better to say, "no probs," or "that's okay," rather than criticise herself.

I like my Mum's cooking, but if I praise her or thank her, she will immediately dismiss what I've said.

She'll compare her cooking to some of the professional chefs that she sees on the TV and think about how mediocre her food is compared to theirs.

That's like going for a run and comparing yourself with Usain Bolt, Michael Johnson, or Mo Farah.

There's no point in doing that, it's far better to graciously accept people's acknowledgement and praise.

When you accept other peoples praise, they usually like that, and it makes them feel better.

If you're always dismissing the kind words that other people say about you, then you're dismissing their opinion, which isn't productive.

If anything, this makes you feel worse and it can make the people giving the praise feel worse. If you always reject peoples praise, then it's likely for them to get to a a stage of thinking, "Why should I even bother saying nice things if they're not going to accept my praise?"

So always accept the praise that is given to you, it will make you feel better and it will make the person who is giving you the praise feel better.

One day I had a phone call from my Son's Mum, and she said that he wanted to talk to me.

Just before he left to go over to his mothers previously I set him a goal of getting a certain amount of points in his spelling game.

I told him that if he went from having 2,300 points to 3,000 points on his spelling game, I would let him take the iPad back over to his Mum's so he could play iPad games over there.

He told me on the phone that had gone from 2,300 points to getting an additional 300 points, which moved him much closer towards his goal of 3,000 points.

I could sense by the tone of his voice that he was delighted with this, and I praised him and said, 'Well done, that's fantastic, I'm very proud of you, my champion!"

Léon was delighted with how I felt about him getting more points and normally after I've spoken to his Mum and I've spoken to him, that would be the end of the phone call, but he asked me if I would like to speak to his Mum again.

I knew that this wasn't normal, but I thought I knew why he wanted me to speak to his Mum again. Before he went over to hand her the phone he said, "What are you going to talk to Mummy about Daddy?"

I told him that I was going to tell her how proud I am of him and I think he is doing fantastically with his spelling game. He handed the phone back to his Mum and went to play on the trampoline.

When Léon gave the phone back to his Mum, she seemed a bit confused why he would give the phone back to her.

I asked her if Léon was still standing next to her, and she said that he'd gone over to play on the trampoline.

I told her that I think he has given the phone back to her because he wanted me to tell her how well he was doing.

I thought that this was brilliant, because I knew that he valued my opinion of him.

I know a lot of children that don't value the opinion of their parents for one reason or another, so it meant a lot to me.

Just as she was about to hang up the phone, I could hear Léon saying in the background, "What did Daddy talk to you about Mummy?"

I remember hanging up with a smile on my face and feeling good because I knew she would tell him about how pleased I was with his progress and I knew that it would make him feel happy and proud.

This is the sort of situation where everybody is a winner. I was happier, my son Léon was happier and if Léon is in a good mood, then that's going to be better for his Mum because she obviously likes to see him happy which would've made her happier!

Praise from others can lift us up, especially in challenging times.

We all need encouragement and support in life and the more you encourage people with kind words and support, the more likely they are to have their spirits lifted.

But there is another benefit to this which is the more you praise them, the more likely they are to help you with whatever goals that you want to achieve.

On the other side of the coin, if you're harsh with someone and you criticise them too much, it will work against you.

So always give praise whenever you can and always be grateful for the praise that you receive off others.

CHAPTER 10

WORDS = POWER

"We are shaped by our thoughts, we become what we think."
Buddha

The words that you think about and say to yourself will give you power.

They can give you power in a positive way or they can lead you down a dark path.

Either way, the words you tell yourself will direct have a bigger impact on how your life turns out than any other factor!

I've never been a fan of saying the words 'I've worked really hard' or 'It'll take hard work.'

I don't like to tell myself something is hard because it gives my mind a psychological disadvantage.

The minute you say something is hard, is when things get even more difficult.

One of my first experiences was when I was on the

Commando Course. Although I was fitter than the average person, this was still in the early days of my fitness, and my fitness was relatively poor compared to the fitness I had when I left the army and did ultra distance running.

When on the 9 mile speed march, I said to myself, "This is horrendous." I can remember the pain in my legs. It was as if my legs filled with lead and because I told myself how hard it was, I struggled even more than was necessary.

In fact I would've probably failed that test if I hadn't turned my mind to saying, "This is easy, this is easy, this is easy, I can do it, I can do it."

Without realising it, many people give themselves psychological disadvantages by using the wrong internal dialogue.

Your self talk is crucial, not only to succeeding with new goals but also to your happiness in life.

What you tell yourself will determine the quality of your life and will determine your mental health!

It's also very common for people to let the weather control their mind more than it should do.

I've seen people that have complained about how hot it is when it's 90°F.

They say things like, "I can't cope in this heat." Little do they know that just by saying these words, it makes them less capable of coping with the heat.

One of the most common things that you see and hear, especially in the UK, is how the rain can affect some people's mindset. "Oh it's a terrible day today isn't it?" they'll say.

The reality is, it's not a terrible day, it's just wet.

These sorts of things should never affect you psychologically!

Yes they can have an effect on you physically, but many people let these conditions affect them more than they should.

I can remember doing a 24 hour run and walk, and within the first couple of hours I got a very dull ache in the side of my knee. There was a part of my mind that was saying to myself, I need to stop now because this could lead to a greater injury.

If you're running through an injury, then it can lead to

massive complications later on down the road.

However, it wasn't a sharp pain in the side of my knee. If it was a sharp pain, that would've been a warning sign, and I would've stopped and pulled out of the challenge.

I kept on running and that dull ache in the side of my left knee disappeared after about six or seven hours of running.

I kept telling myself that it was nothing but a minor inconvenience, which became the reality.

There's also been times when my books haven't been selling as fast as I would've liked, which is something that most authors will go through no matter how successful they are.

It would be very easy for me to talk myself out of carrying on, but it's something that I love doing. If I gave up with my books because things weren't happening fast enough, it would be ironic, because I would not be taking my own advice in the books.

Fortunately, the more books that I put out there, the more success I had, which motivated me even more.

Some of the most troublesome times for us can be when

we aren't progressing as fast as we would like to. The dangerous part comes when we stop taking action towards our goals and start telling ourselves that there is no point in carrying on.

It's much easier to take the easy way out than it is to carry on through the most difficult times.

You need an attitude that says, "Bring it on!"

I watched a great movie one day with my Mum about the successful baseball player called Jackie Robinson.

Jackie was the first black man to play professional baseball at the highest level, and this was back in the day when racism was a lot more rife. He suffered death threats and was under relentless verbal attack from fans and players.

However, Jackie rose above it and became an inspiration, not only for black people around the world but a massive inspiration for people of all different races, colour, religion and cultures.

Human beings naturally sway to negative self talk much easier than they do to positive self talk, so it will take a level of effort to change your negative self talk into positive self talk.

The first and the most important step to changing your negative thinking is to realise that you are doing it.

The second step is to understand that you can change it.

The third step is to focus on the activity that you want to do, and tell yourself that you are not only capable of achieving it, but you are superb at it!

When you talk to yourself you need to say phrases such as:

- I am a winner.
- I am confident.
- I am strong.
- I am a machine.
- I always win in the end.
- Nothing can stop me.
- I am achieving great things.

It's all well and good saying,

"I'll try"

or

"I will"

But you need to talk positively to yourself 'in the present' which will make you a stronger person.

Say the words,

"I am"

and follow those words by saying what you want to be or achieve.

No matter how many failures you've gone through, now is the time to pick yourself back up and tell yourself the truth.

And the truth is, you are a winner!

Just by reading this book, you're already showing that you want to change your life for the better.

You've got to put the effort in and take action, because when you do this, your chances of success increase massively!

If you don't take any action, then you've already failed, but that failure doesn't need to be final.

Hopefully, you'll find most of this book useful, but if you're only going to take one thing out of this book, then take this,

"THE WORDS YOU CHOOSE WILL DECIDE WHETHER YOU WIN OR LOSE!"

CHAPTER 11

MOVING SWIFTLY TOWARDS YOUR DREAMS

"Patience, persistence and perspiration make an unbeatable combination for success."

Napoleon Hill

On the 13th December 1989, a baby girl was born in Reading, Pennsylvania, USA.

When she was a teenager, she convinced her parents to support her with her goal of becoming a country and western singer.

They believed in her and wanted the very best for their daughter, so they moved to Nashville when she was only 13 years old with a dream of getting a record deal.

Her mum travelled with her whenever she had a gig and would routinely fall asleep on aeroplanes and in rental cars due to the travelling schedule.

However, her Mum wanted the best for her daughter, so she was relentless in helping her little girl get to where she wanted to go.

The young girl's initial goal was to meet and work with

songwriters; especially the ones who wrote the kind of songs that got stuck in your head.

She wanted to know, 'What made a hit song a hit?'

The young songwriter persisted and eventually at the age of just 14 years old, she signed a publishing deal and became a songwriter with Sony.

Her commitment to her chosen career path impressed her elder colleagues so much that it opened up more doors for her.

This lead to working with established songwriters she really respected.

She was still studying at school at this time, but as soon as she got home from her lessons, her song writing took over!

I have found that this is not an uncommon trait with successful people; their careful time management allows them to live an almost 'double-life' until their true vocation can financially sustain them.

The young songwriter ended up staying in Nashville for two and a half years.

At only 15 years old, she was offered a golden opportunity with an artist development deal with RCA (Radio Corporation of America).

This was a huge thing and many people would've been delighted with something like that, but the catch was they wanted her to work for them with no definite deal in place at the end of it.

However, even at 15 years old she knew what she wanted to achieve and turned down RCA, which completely shocked the corporate bosses.

She described the proposed deal as "Kind of like a guy that wanted to date you but didn't want you to be his girlfriend."

She wanted more commitment from RCA, but it wasn't to be.

Not long after turning down RCA, the young girl did a performance at the small and intimate Bluebird café when she caught the eye of Scott Borchetta, who had recently started a small independent record label company.

Although many people in the Country and Western music industry at that time didn't think she was going to achieve anything significant, Borchetta could see her young talent shining bright and wanted to sign her to his fledgling label.

When he pitched his request to her, he agreed to let her write and sing the songs she wanted to, as well as letting her be involved in the production aspect within the studio.

This meant she had almost full control of her music. Such freedom was music to the singer songwriter's ears and she signed the contract.

Signing for a small independent label that offered her freedom rather than signing for a large label (that would have controlled her more) was a huge turning point in her career!

I've also seen this with authors.

Some people have become successful by signing a traditional publishing deal with the big top five publishers (Penguin Random House, HarperCollins, Hachette, Simon and Schuster and Macmillan).

As cool as this is, there are huge numbers of authors who have signed with the big companies that haven't made a very successful career of being an author.

On the other side of the coin, I have also seen indie (independent) published authors (or self published authors) that have not had a successful career as an author.

However, there are also massively successful Indy authors that have published lots of books and make six figure and seven figure annual incomes.

In other words, there is more than one way to be successful!

The young girl was a massive Country and Western fan and had already written a song called 'Tim McGraw' when she was younger.

In the United States, Tim McGraw is a hugely successful Country and Western singer so Borchetta and the young girl decided to bring that track out as her first officially released single.

The addition of Tim McGraw's name on the single attracted a tremendous amount of attention and brought the young girl's voice to the attention of a large Country and Western audience.

It was pure marketing genius and was a big hit!

The music press called her the next Shania Twain, and believed she could cross over from country style music to the mainstream pop charts.

From that point on she kept having hit single after hit single with her first album.

One of the songs on the album was called 'Teardrops On My Guitar,' which was a very personal song to her about somebody she used to fancy but things never went anywhere because he had a girlfriend.

The song connected on a deep level with the audience and this 'connecting' became something she would try to do with most of her songs.

When she went through personal disappointments, she ended up writing about them and turned them into hit songs.

It's often that way in life where you can take something that's a negative situation and turn it into something positive. And if that positive thing helps other people, then even better!

The little girl had come a long way from where she started.

Sometimes when we see a young person become famous we think it was all done overnight, but the reality with this girl was she had been writing songs from an early age.

She was very prolific and wrote lots of songs.

In other words, she had been working on her craft for years and years before she became successful enough to do what she loved full time.

At the time of writing, she is still only 30 years old, and is reported to have written over 200 songs with around half of them making it onto her albums.

According to Wikipedia, her 2006 debut album was the longest charting album of the 2000s in the US.

The third single she released made her the youngest person to write and perform a Number 1 song on the Billboard Hot Country Songs chart.

She crossed over into popular chart music in 2008 and her second album became the best selling US album of 2009, which was certified 'Diamond' (more than 10 million sales).

Her second album won four Grammy Awards including

Album of the Year.

At the time of writing she:

- Has won 10 Grammy Awards.
- Has won an Emmy Award.
- Has six Guinness World Records.
- Has been honoured by the Songwriters Hall of Fame.
- Has been included in the Rolling Stone Magazine '100 Greatest Song Writers of all Time' list in 2015.
- Was ranked first in the 'Forbes Celebrity 100' in both 2016 and 2019.
- Has sold more than 50 million albums worldwide.
- Is one of the world's best selling music artists.

The young country girl worked her ass off, gave value, and provided entertainment to millions of people around the world.

Her name is Taylor Swift!

One of the things Taylor was extremely good at was getting around the right people.

She heard an Ed Sheeran song (when he wasn't as well known in the US) and loved it.

After meeting him and finding out how down-to-earth he was, she asked him if he would go on tour with her in the United States.

He replied yes and his live audience in the U.S. went from 5,000 people to stadiums of 50,000 – 100,000 people.

Taylor said,

"When it comes to touring with people, I've learned over the years, it's very important that they are good on stage but it's almost more important that they are a fit off stage. With Ed it was like having a little Labrador puppy scampering around backstage. He was talking to everybody; he became best friends with everyone on the tour. He'd do karaoke parties after the show with the dancers, he'd go and hang out with the band afterwards, and he'd go for a beer with the crew. Everyone loved him and it made everyone happier, and when everyone is happier it makes for a more seamless tour."

When Taylor did an interview called '73 questions with Taylor Swift' for Vogue, she was asked, "What's one thing you still have from your childhood?" to which she replied: "My insecurities."

In other words, it doesn't matter how successful somebody becomes, they can still have doubts and insecurities.

If someone has never had any doubts or insecurities, that's simply because they haven't lived life enough because life will always test you. It will at times, test you to your core and it will rip you apart and spit you out!

The good news is, you can battle through your insecurities and doubts and gain confidence to create an amazing life for yourself and your loved ones.

When I watched an interview with Taylor, I could tell her heart was in the right place, especially when the interviewer asked her "If you had a superpower, what would it be?"

She replied, "Healing people."

While I was typing these words, I asked my 10 year old son Léon what his favourite superpower would be.

He said that his favourite superpower would be that me (his Dad), his Mummy and everyone he cared about stayed alive forever.

I thought "Oh what a sweet little angel."

He then said, (in a sweet way) "But everyone that's naughty, they can die!"

I have to admit I burst out laughing and he just looked at me and said, "Yeah but they deserve it."

Priceless!

When Taylor was asked, "What is the most important life lesson someone can learn?" she replied: "Karma is real."

Taylor also took bold moves with her music career and had some unlikely collaborations.

One of those was with British rock band Def Leppard which is her mum's favourite band. The public loved it!

She reportedly has a sign on her tour bus that says, "Never ever give up!"

Even with all of the success and fame she's also managed to remain very grateful, and down-to-earth; and that of course is part of her appeal to the public.

Taylor also credits her success down to all of her team and people that have helped her on her journey.

Here are some of the things that we can learn from the Taylor Swift success story:

- Believe in yourself.
- Believe in your dreams.
- Surround yourself with positive people who support you.
- Give your team and supporters credit along your journey.
- Know what steps you need to take and turn those steps into a habit.
- Dream big.
- You will always get failures in life so keep going!
- Try to connect with people on a deep level.
- Be bold.
- Set short-term attainable goals.

- Stand your ground and stick to your own principles.
- Be willing to think outside the box.
- Stay humble.
- We all get hurt but we can get back up and live a great life.
- Always look for ways to improve things.
- Collaborate with other successful people.
- Be grateful.
- Keep going through the tough times.
- No matter who you are you will always get people that are critical of what you do.
- You can still have insecurities at times, no matter how successful or confident you are.
- What you send out comes back to you – Karma is real.
- Turn negative situations into positive situations.

- Be nice to people.

- Never ever give up!

CHAPTER 12

CONFIDENCE COMES FROM PUTTING THE WORK IN

"I must lose myself in action, least I weather in despair."
Alfred Lord Tennyson

The quote above from Tennyson is very powerful because it states if you don't put in the work, then you will have little confidence and doubt your abilities.

Tennyson became The Poet Laureate (succeeding William Wordsworth) of the United Kingdom, which is an honorary position given to him by Queen Victoria. This honorary position doesn't have any specific duties other than the person who holds the position is expected to write a poem on significant national occasions.

For his work, Tennyson was awarded the Chancellor's Gold Medal at Cambridge.

Some of his most notable short lyrics were, 'Break, Break, Break,' 'Crossing the Bar,' and 'The Charge of the Light Brigade.'

Tennyson's phrases from his work have also become famous throughout the world, such as:

"Tis better to have loved and lost, than never to have loved at all."

And,

"Theirs not to reason why, theirs but to do and die."

Tennyson became successful because he knew how important it was to take action and put the work in!

When I broke the 100 kilometre treadmill world record, I was asked by news reporter Kate Evans Hughes if I felt confident I would break the world record. The TV cameras were rolling, so the words that came out of my mouth were important because I would have to live with what I said in public.

But they weren't just important for that reason, they were important to me because I needed to believe that I was going to smash the record.

My reply to Kate was, "As long as I don't get injured, the record will go!"

She looked at me, smiled and said, "You're confident then?"

I smiled and nodded.

This may seem a little cocky, but two weeks before I took on the 100k record, I had already run a 50k at the same pace that I was going to run the 100k.

When I got off the treadmill after finishing the 50k training run, I knew the run didn't make me tired in the slightest. That gave me a massive amount of confidence going into the 100k!

But even before I got to the 50k training run, I had already put a tremendous amount of running time in. What gave me even more confidence was I had already beaten the current world record holder at a 50 mile race in the Sahara desert.

In that 50 mile race, I crossed the finish line about an hour and a half before he did. So that gave me even more confidence.

If you've put the work in, it will give you a lot of confidence when the time comes to perform on the day!

However, if you don't put the training in, or if you don't put the work in, when the time of your competition arrives, or your deadline for a certain piece of work arrives, then it will be highlighted for all to see!

As simple as it may sound, you have to tell yourself that

you are good at what you do and you have to convince yourself that you are going to be successful. There will be moments of doubt that creep in from time to time, but the best cure for doubt is taking action!

You may work towards a goal that hasn't got a specific deadline on it and you're not under any pressure. However, what you have or haven't done will show up sooner or later.

Let's look at my own example.

At the current time, I am writing a series of books. If these books don't get produced it might not mean that much to anybody else, but it makes a difference to me. Maybe not immediately, maybe not in a few months time, maybe not in a few years time, but at the end of my life it will be massively highlighted.

I don't know about you, but I want to look back and think, "I've put the effort in and it paid off big style!"

When you know you've put the effort in, and you achieve your goals you will gain more and more confidence. Every little success, no matter how small, will add to your confidence.

Because one of my goals is to have a lot of books

published and be a very successful author, just the fact that I'm writing these words down gives me more confidence.

Writing a few sentences or paragraphs down might seem like a long way off having many books published, but it's those little steps that create something significant.

It's also important to remember, when you're going through the necessary steps to making your goal a reality, you don't become overwhelmed by the process.

Yes it may be slow going and yes you may want more success faster, but you've just got to keep grinding it out, because the people that grind it out are the people who are the most successful in life!

You don't want to be left thinking, "If only I put more effort in, I could've made it!"

Or

"My life could be so much better if I didn't give up so soon."

Think about your own goals and dreams you want to achieve. Because, when you can't be bothered to do what needs to be done, the person who has to motivate you the most, and kick your arse into taking action the most, is you.

So go out there, put the time into your dream, and never give up!

CHAPTER 13

HABITS

"Excellence comes about as a result of habit."
Aristotle

In many ways, becoming a successful author it is a lot tougher than many jobs I've had or an elite military course such as the Commando Course.

The reason for this is that when you're an indie author like me, and you haven't got a massive following, you have to motivate yourself all the time.

If you're someone who just loves writing all the time, and there's nothing else you ever want to do apart from marketing and all of that kind of stuff that goes along with being an indie author, then things are a lot easier.

However, if you're more like me, where some days you don't want to do any writing, marketing and learning new things about the business, then it can be more challenging.

When you're putting the work in to achieving your goals, there may be some days when you just want to sit down, watch the TV, eat junk food and chill out.

If you're like this, then don't worry, because this is a very natural way to think and sometimes we just need to unplug and have some downtime for ourselves.

When we unplug and have downtime, it can stop us from getting burned out.

And sometimes you need to recharge your own physical and mental batteries.

When you're on a military course like the Commando Course, you wake up and you're around your friends or colleagues who will help motivate you.

If they don't help motivate you, then the staff on the training team will.

You're given set tasks to do each day and you go out there and do them even though they can be very challenging.

Whereas if you're an entrepreneur or an author (unless you have a ghostwriter to work with), you're just there on your own and there's nobody to tell you to do something.

You have to be the one to motivate yourself and put the effort in!

It's the same thing with running. Only you can motivate

yourself and the easiest way to get good at something like ultra distance running or being a successful at anything for that matter is to do it a lot.

The more you get into the habit of doing it regularly, the easier it becomes. The less you do, the more difficult things are!

So every day TAKE ACTION and CREATE A HABIT for your goals!

Yes, it's going to be hard at times, but you're strong enough to go through those tough times and succeed!

If what you're doing isn't tough at times, then it may not even be worthwhile.

When things are handed to us on a plate, we are less likely to feel grateful for those things but when we have strived incredibly hard and put a lot of hours into something, we are far more likely to gain more confidence and have a greater sense of pride.

Successful people are those people that keep on doing the basics again, and again, and again.

Most of the time it's not glamorous, or pretty. Most of the time it's just you, your thoughts, and you putting in the work to make yourself a success!

So create the habit of doing something every day that you can. Yes, have the odd day off, but make sure that you get back into the swing of things without taking too much time off.

It's also very important to focus on your purpose, on why you're doing what you're doing.

Maybe you're putting effort into something because:

- You want to be in better shape.
- You want to create a better future for your family.
- You want to have more time off work in a few years time.
- You want to have more choices in your life.
- You want to achieve something great.
- You want to prove that you are more than what others think of you.

Whatever the reason is, it's vital that you focus on that reason because that reason will give you the drive and the motivation to create a habit.

EPILOGUE

"There is no elevator to success, you have to take the stairs."
Zig Ziglar

One of the things that I did with this book was I deliberately created the chapters at different lengths.

In almost every book you will come across, chapters usually have a similar length. They can be 500 words long, they can be 1,000 words long, they can be 2,000 words long or they can be up to 4,000 words long.

The chapter that you read earlier on Arnold Schwarzenegger was over 5,000 words long.

This is much longer than the average chapter and even longer than a 'long chapter' when it comes to writing books.

If you got through that chapter, congratulations, you clearly have the ability to keep going, even when you might have expected the goal to be reached in less time and with less effort.

The reason that I varied the lengths of each chapter is because, when I feel that I've written enough information on a certain chapter, I'll finish the chapter. But also, the chapter length relates to life. And the truth, as you probably already know, is that life is full of variations and life is not predictable.

The only predictable things in life are:

- We'll all leave this physical body one day.

And

- Change is inevitable.

When I was on the Commando Course, a little trick the training team used to pull sometimes was, we would be on a long march or a run, and we would be told that the finish point is where the four ton vehicle is.

Sometimes, we would get to the four ton vehicle thinking we were at the finish, and it would drive off.

I could see this suck the life out of some people, I could see that they had a guts full and because of this, some people even wanted to quit.

Personally, I didn't give two fucks when that lorry drove

off!

I might have been cold, I might have been tired, I might have been hungry, but I always thought those mind games from the training team were part of the game.

And no one was going to stop me!

That's the mindset you need if you were going to succeed at something important.

When you think that you're getting to the end and you're just about to achieve your goal, that goal and timeframe can be moved.

If you ever played a sport like rugby or American football, then you'll know there can be times when you kick the ball and the wind will take it off in a different direction.

You've kicked the ball with enough power, your shot on goal is extremely accurate, but in the last nanosecond, a gust of wind takes the ball off course and you miss the goal.

That's what life can do to us sometimes!

You've probably noticed the same thing happens with other aspects of life when it's not necessarily goal orientated towards achieving something.

People can be unpredictable, one minute they can be great and the next minute they can be a complete **** (fill in the blank yourself).

You have to adjust in life and keep going!

When the wind of life hits you, you'll be blown from side to side, but ultimately, you just have to keep your head down, with your eyes looking up and focusing on the destination that you want to get to.

Remember…

You are stronger than any challenge that can be thrown your way!

You are destined for great things!

So be bold, take action and live the life of your dreams!

"People are illogical, unreasonable, and self-centred.
Love them anyway.
If you do good, people will accuse you of selfish ulterior motives.
Do good anyway.
If you are successful, you will win false friends and
true enemies.
Succeed anyway.
The good you do today will be forgotten tomorrow.
Do good anyway.
Honesty and frankness make you vulnerable.
Be honest and frank anyway.
The biggest men and women with the biggest ideas can be shot
down by the smallest men and women with the smallest minds.
Think big anyway.
People favour underdogs but follow only top dogs.
Fight for a few underdogs anyway.
What you spend years building may be destroyed overnight.
Build anyway.
People really need help but may attack you if you do help them.
Help people anyway.
Give the world the best you have and you'll get kicked in
the teeth.
Give the world the best you have anyway."

– Kent M. Keith

ACKNOWLEDGEMENTS

It's almost impossible to say how many people have helped me along the way with producing this book, and if you're not in the acknowledgements just know that I am very grateful for your support and help.

However, I would like to say a massive THANK YOU to a few people that I can think of, off the top of my head:

Paul 'The Viking' Hughes, Tom Webb, Eva Savage, Mark 'Billy' Billingham, Julie Colombino-Billingham, Tracy, Kay and Maria Morris, Cheryl Hicks, Jamie Baulch, Gene Hipgrave, Tom Hughes, Kauri-Romet Aadamsoo, Mark Dawson, Craig Martelle, Michael Anderle, Michael and Emma Byrne, Paul 'Faz' Farrington, Paul Heaney, James Atkinson and Laura Taylor.

Also, a huge THANKS to 'The Mark Llewhellin Advance Reader Team' for taking the time to read the manuscript and make suggestions.

Live Your Dreams!

Mark

ABOUT THE AUTHOR

In 1990, Mark Llewhellin left school without knowing his grades. He had little confidence and was not at all optimistic about his future.

Not knowing what to do with his life Mark followed some of his friends into the Army. He failed his basic 1.5-mile run, was bullied, and was also voted the fattest person in the Troop!

After a year with the Junior Leaders Regiment Royal Artillery, Mark decided he would try and get into 29 Commando Regiment Royal Artillery, which is an elite Army Commando Regiment that at the time proudly held the Military Marathon World Record (i.e. a marathon carrying a 40lbs backpack).

After failing the 29 Commando Selection phase (called 'The Beat Up') twice, first through lack of fitness and secondly through an injury, Mark subsequently passed on his third attempt and completed the 'All Arms Commando Course' on his first attempt.

Mark later went on to achieve the following:

- Break the 100 kilometre Treadmill World Record.

- Place 1st in the Strava Distance Challenge in 2015 competing against over 51,000 runners.

- Place 1st in the Strava Distance Challenge in 2014 competing against over 40,000 runners.

- Run and walk 70 miles without training on his 40th birthday.

- Become a successful Personal Fitness Trainer.

- Complete the Marathon Des Sables (a six-day, 135-mile ultra-marathon in the Sahara Desert).

- Work and live in London's exclusive Park Lane as a Bodyguard.

- Run 1,620 miles in the United States whilst carrying a 35lbs pack.

Mark has interviewed some of the world's top performers and high achievers in various locations, including one of the world's most prestigious memorabilia rooms…the Hard Rock Café Vault Room in London.

He has travelled to over 50 countries and has been featured in leading national newspapers and on TV for his running achievements.

Mark has extensively worked in the support and care industry for many years helping individuals with brain injury, autism, epilepsy, dyspraxia, and various types of learning difficulties.

He is the Managing Director of Mark 7 Productions, as well as the Producer and Host of 'An Audience with Mark Billy Billingham' speaking events around the UK.

Mark is currently working on more personal development books and lives with his son Léon (when Léon's not at his Mum's) on a beautiful marina in South West Wales.

ALSO BY MARK LLEWHELLIN

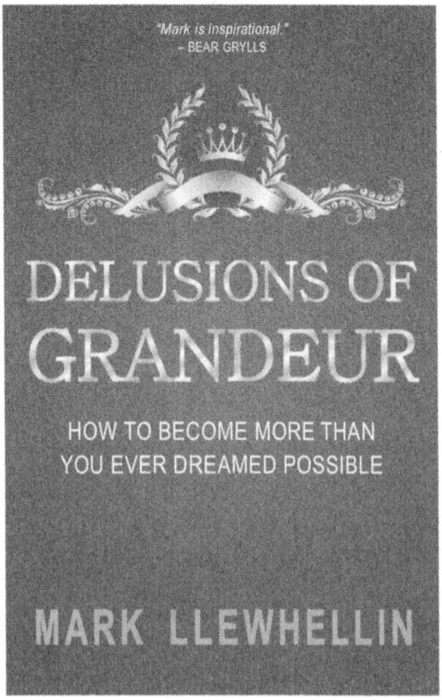

IF YOU ENJOYED THIS BOOK

Your help in spreading the word about Mark's books is greatly appreciated and your reviews make a huge difference to help new readers change their lives for the better.

If you found this book useful please leave a review on the platform you purchased it on.

MARK LLEWHELLIN BOOKS OUT IN 2020

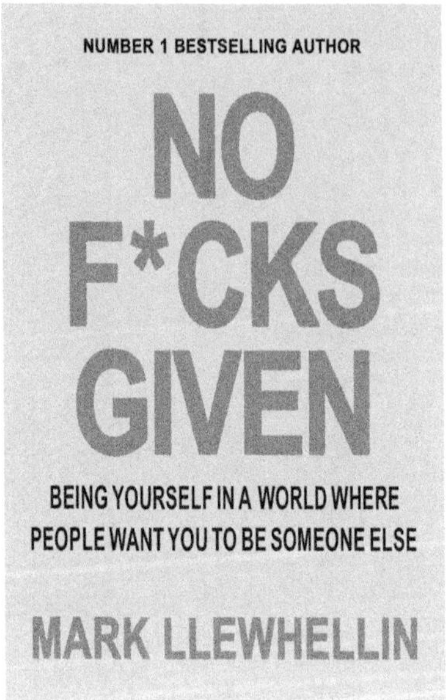

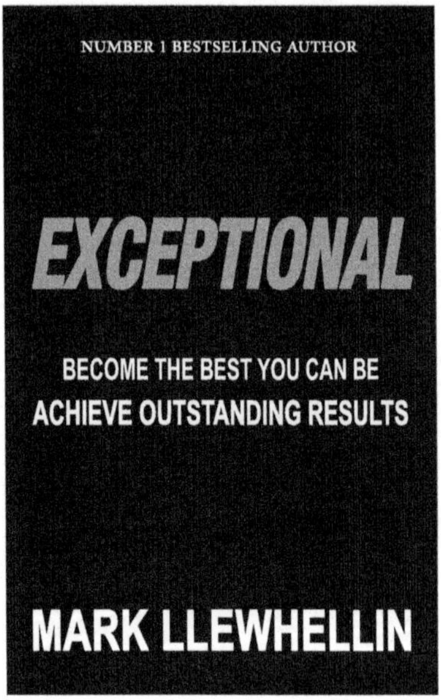

GET TWO FREE MARK LLEWHELLIN BOOKS AND DEALS AND UPDATES

Join 'The Mark Llewhellin Advance Reader Team' for information on new books and deals plus:

You can pick up FREE copies of Mark's five star reviewed books:

1. 'The Underdog'

2. 'Delusions of Grandeur'

Simply go to Mark's website at www.markllewhellin.com and sign up for FREE.

REFERENCES

National Geographic

Amazon Prime

Netflix

YouTube

Disney +

Total Recall by Arnold Schwarzenegger

Taylor Swift – America sweetheart

Taylor Swift: From The Heart

Statista

The orchard on demand

Brainy Quote

Oxford dictionary

Cambridge dictionary

DISCLAIMER

Although the author and publisher have made every effort to ensure that the information contained in this book was accurate at the time of release, the author and publisher do not assume and hereby disclaim any liability to any party for any loss, damage, or disruption caused by errors or omissions in this book, whether such errors or omissions result from negligence, accident, or any other cause.

A Mark 7 Publications Paperback.

First published in Great Britain in 2020

by Mark 7 Publications

ISBN 978-0-9956501-7-6

Book design and formatting by Tom Webb
pixelfiddler@hotmail.co.uk

Printed in Great Britain
by Amazon

48007245R00108